LIFE
THROUGH
Quotes

DR. ABHIMANYU KAURA

First Published in April 2023

ISBN: 978-93-5741-517-0

BLUEROSE PUBLISHERS
www.BlueRoseONE.com
info@bluerosepublishers.com
+91 8882 898 898

Cover Design:
Aman Sharma

Typographic Design:
Namrata Saini

Distributed by: BlueRose, Amazon, Flipkart

NOT FOR EVERYONE

IF on this earth with 6 billion others , u still
feel alone
Just remember that all the stars u see
always carry u along
Earth is not the place where u belong

U were born deep inside the universe
billions of years ago
Here it is just a phase , so let it come and
go

 Here on this earth don't expect anything
from anyone
thats why I gave u all the 9 planets , the
moons and the sun
So always remember u r not for everyone.

I want to tell you how important you are
Go out and look at the stars

You can't even see them all
May be you are not that tall

But every single star is watching you
Is that not enough for you

Sometimes 1 is better than 2

you are always living in past
and future, with each second
you are travelling in future,
from past to future.

theoritically there is no
present because time never
stops.

being present can be a state
of mind but it cannot be a
state of time.

being humble is not that easy,

even showing that you don't

show off is also a kind of show

off

half of your ego
comes from what you
are not.

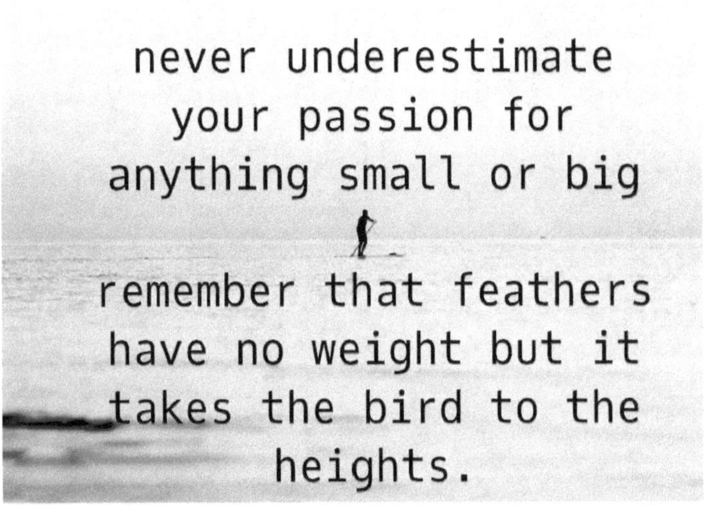

never underestimate
your passion for
anything small or big

remember that feathers
have no weight but it
takes the bird to the
heights.

IN ORDER
TO MAKE
YOUR
IDENTITY ,
YOU HAVE
TO LOOSE
IT FIRST.

understand
one should ~~read~~ a book

read
and ~~understand~~ the
people

believe in yourself until you are wrong.

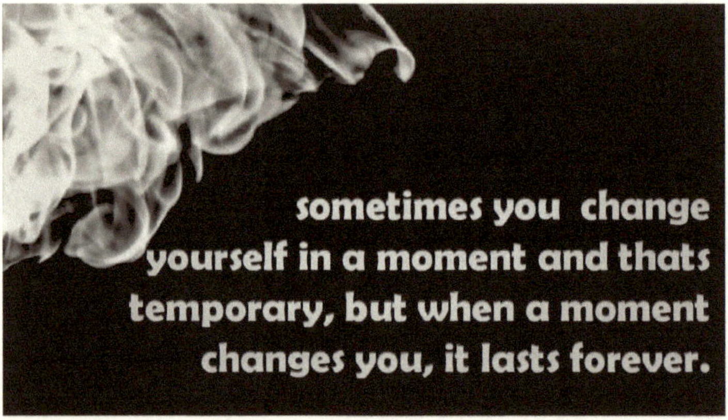

sometimes you change
yourself in a moment and thats
temporary, but when a moment
changes you, it lasts forever.

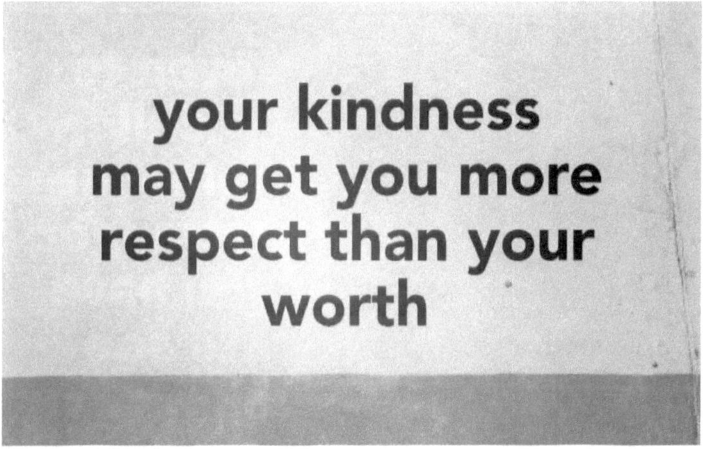

your kindness
may get you more
respect than your
worth

even to
call
someone
a stranger,
you have
to see
them once

apology is always

heavier than the

guilt

Only 1 from the 100 million cells fought to become you. Now continue that legacy.

Right moment never come
before right decision.

people often avoid
you just to save you.

your real
journey starts
when you
don't know
where to go

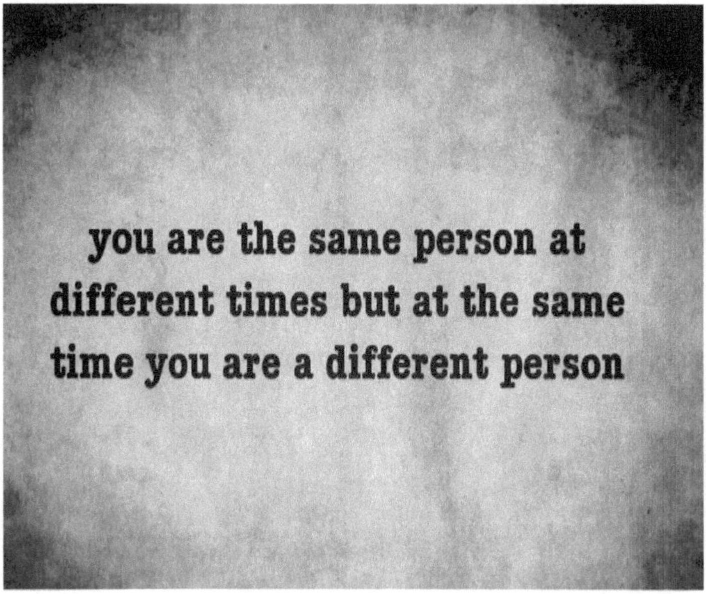

you are the same person at
different times but at the same
time you are a different person

people generally
don't repeat what
they regret but they
keep repeating the
regret

i never ask anyone
how are you because
i know except me
everyone is fine

nothing in this
universe can create
as much chaos as
the collision of two
thoughts.

life never gives you
choice, it gives
you freedom.

You are not always reusable, but you make yourself

SOME PEOPLE EVEN CARRY THE
BURDEN OF SAYING "NO"

what you write,
writes you.

that which can
only be given
and can never
be taken is
love .

no one can
inspire you,
motivate you.
In reality you
can only be
entertained.

*everything comes
with peace and
goes with it.*

go and fulfill them, if you
know that someone have
some expectation from you.
because most expectations
are never too big.

everyone is unique in
their own way.
your

*everything makes sense to a
disturbed mind.*

from pleasing
others to
loosing self is
the journey
of a selfish
person.

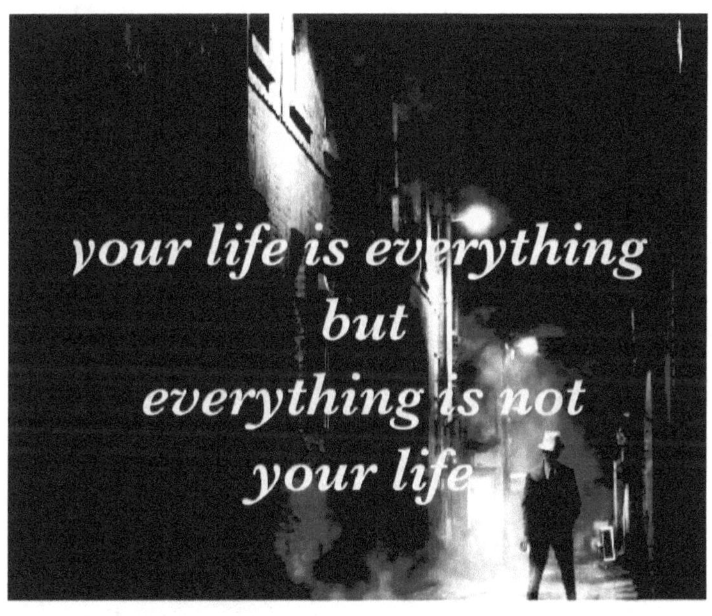

your life is everything
but
everything is not
your life

complicated

you cannot ignore
someone who is
already ignoring
you.

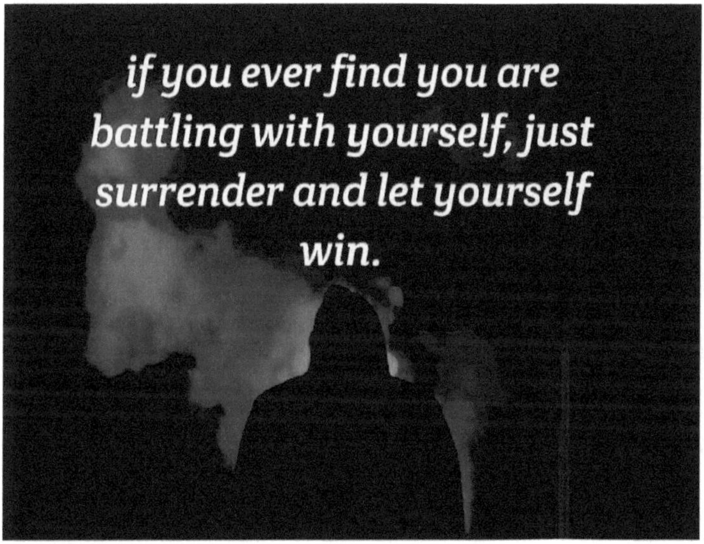

*if you ever find you are
battling with yourself, just
surrender and let yourself
win.*

you hardly judge
yourself because you
know it doesn't matter,
same is the case when
you judge others.

a person giving you
sincere advice is actually
attempting to correct his
past once again.

DIFFERENCE

How much u have gone through ?
For simply being true
U think u r great, u think u know the world
Then u suffer, because actually the world
knows u
So put on the mask like everyone do
Now the difference is u r good from inside
too

Whatever u do is not your karma, your

intention behind is your karma

Don't forget that majority of the people

help the poor only to post that on

social media

And always remember that you can

help someone as quietly as you

perform your sins.

never play what you are not

when everyone is playing
who they are.

your silence will
only matter if your
words did.

your own absence
leads to lonliness.

Always remember

That closest person to you is just like a
treasure you have found
But always remember
Only that person is capable to give you
thd deepest wound
If he or she leaves you in your difficult
time
That is when you have to learn to say that
you are fine.
Always remember
Not to cry
You were born to fly high in the sky.

Harsh Truth

In a relationship, never seek love because love changes with time , although u can't mesure love but still sometimes you feel its more sometimes its less .
 I tell you honesty and loyality are much more important than love.

Never mess your life in search of the
meaning of life.
What you already know is enough.

Your identity is a myth as your whole life is mainly focused on playing what you are not.

What you are not going through should

never bother you.

Nature has put all emotions in each creature of earth like love, hate , anger , fear, kindness. None of the emotions are good or bad. They are not even meant to be controlled.
They are just meant to be understood and observed.

HARSH TRUTH

Reset your goal if you always think you
need motivation to achieve that goal.
When you are clear about your goal then
you don't need any motivation or drama,
you only need action.
Only your goal should be your driving force.
The need of motivation is the first hurdle in
path towards your goal.

Glad to know that you often agree with
yourself when confirmed by others.

Everything is predictable just before a surprise.

The beauty of friendships in this
generation lies in the fact that the 2 words
use and misuse means same here.

A man completes himself by his promises
and establish himself when he keeps them.

In some situations never make your
answer an excuse by giving explanation,
even if it is an excuse.
For a wise man answer is self explanatory
and for great minds, they never think
beyond the answer.
For fools , they will ask a question and
answer themselve.

Remember always

" You will be ignored as soon as you give importance and also when you try to become important. "
                              - Be Real

Be Rational

Always try to be as rational as possible, as by default we all were born to be rational. But society programmed us to think according to their different belief systems.

When you are happy , keep it to yourself
and be natural but don't try to show people
that you are happy.
People have right to question everything
even your happiness.

*speak only a part of what
all you think and write only
what others can't even think*

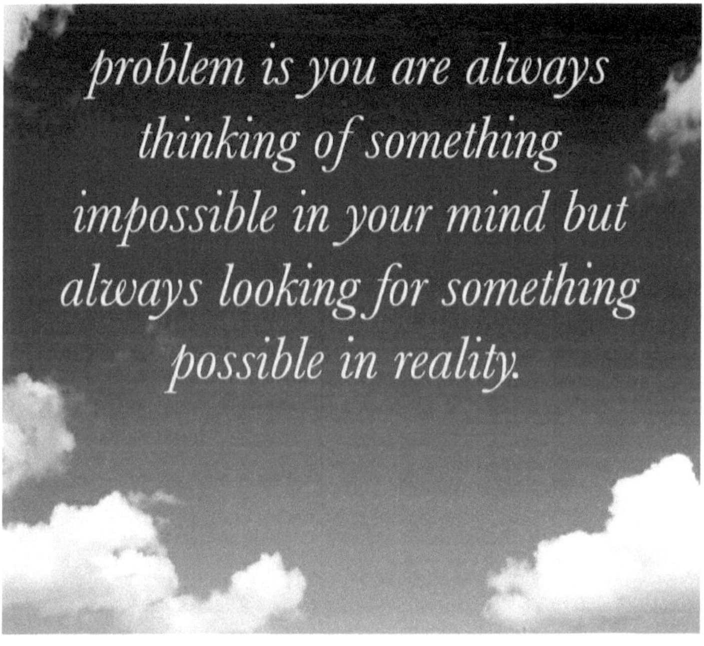

problem is you are always
thinking of something
impossible in your mind but
always looking for something
possible in reality.

depth of sacrifice
defines the depth of a
relationship

Whatever that reminds me about you, is the amount of you left in me.
Whatever that does not remind me about you is left with you.

Either you break the norms
or the norms break you.

hope can be a beautiful
lie

but a lie can never be a
hope

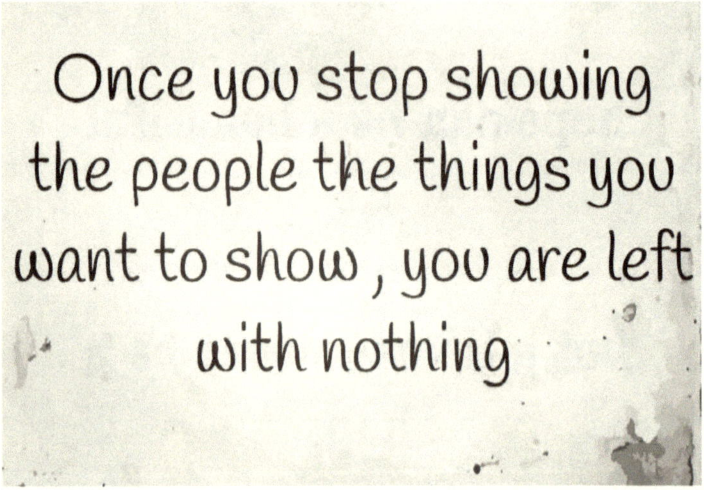

Once you stop showing
the people the things you
want to show , you are left
with nothing

Anything dragged
for too long
becomes a joke.

There is no path,
only diversions

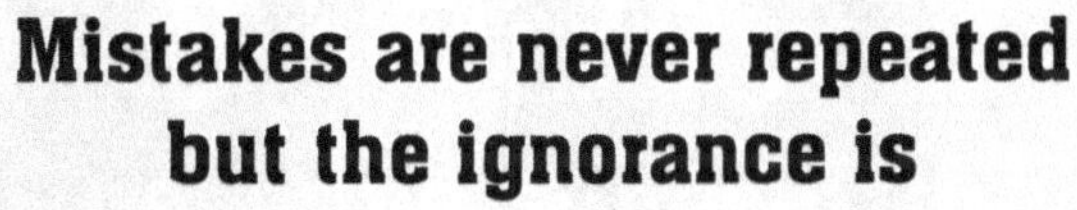

Mistakes are never repeated
but the ignorance is

you are the only
difference between
philosophy and reality.

You probably can do anything
until you know your talent and
after that you are bound to it.

unfortunately its
never about god,
its always about
decoration of
belief.

Genuine people get most of the promises

no pain is better
than any gain.

no gain is better
than any pain.

i don't know how but
meaning remains
the same

except those who don't care,
everyone acquire the art of
making anyone hear without
saying anything.

WANT

YOU NEVER DESERVE WHAT YOU WANT
YOU ALWAYS DESERVE WHAT YOU LOOK
FOR

In life you need only 2 kinds of people ,
one who believe in you and the one who
STILL believe in you.

In life , how much you have lost is always
less than why you have lost.

You cannot run from yourself, even if you
run , you only have one direction which
leads to you only.

you often look at
your past, its
natural. But don't
live it.

Lucky you are if you have
plenty of time but make sure
it's not for waiting

exceptions are more
common, in space.

Talent is not always understood but excellence is visible.

Everything that you can think is happening somewhere in the universe.

You can never know yourself. You can only know what you are not.

The reality is you never loose hope, you
always loose will.

*there can also be one more great
day in your wonderful life, that
day is when you realize that some
people's innocence is limited to
only some people.*

always remember

you get cheated by a person twice
because the first time it was theirs
and second time it was your choice

have courage , you can
even bend the time
before it bends you.

Don't get fooled by the thought or words like "don't judge" .
They come only after you have done that.

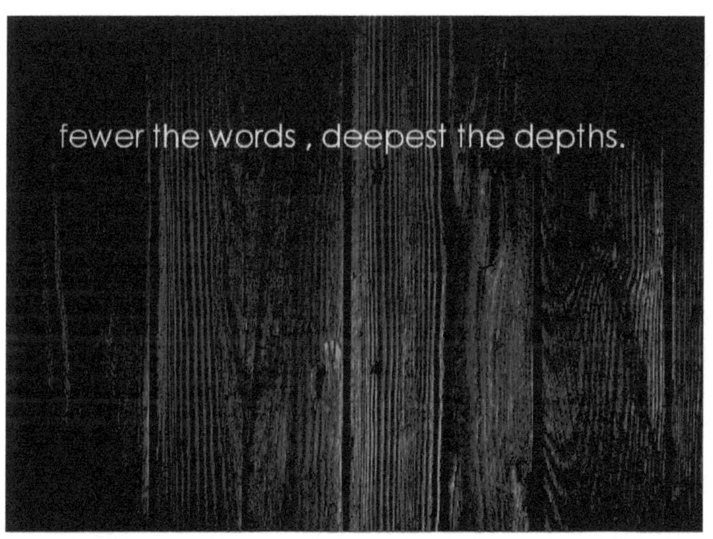
fewer the words , deepest the depths.

today's excuses are
tommorow's realities

silence of
others is the
price of your
words

YOU HAVE TO
ACCEPT YOURSELF
AS YOU ARE TO
ACCEPT THE PEOPL
AS THEY ARE

Whether you like it or you don't, either it is good or it is bad, your past and present have only the potential to become a memory not the future.

some of your enemies
know you better than
your friends

**Some people forget
you if you have not
done anything for
them and also if you
have done
everything for them**

Always choose wisely, its your goal,
destiny and your purpose which makes
you the person you are.

Never forget

your reality is based on the lies you are living.

Either you own a thought
Or
A thought owns you

so as the people
of a country,
so will be the
government.

You don't choose people in your life , they choose you.

Mistakes are mistakes. But only you know that most of the time you make a mistake while thinking not to repeat it again.

Think before you speak
Observe before you think
Be aware before you observe
Be present before you become aware.

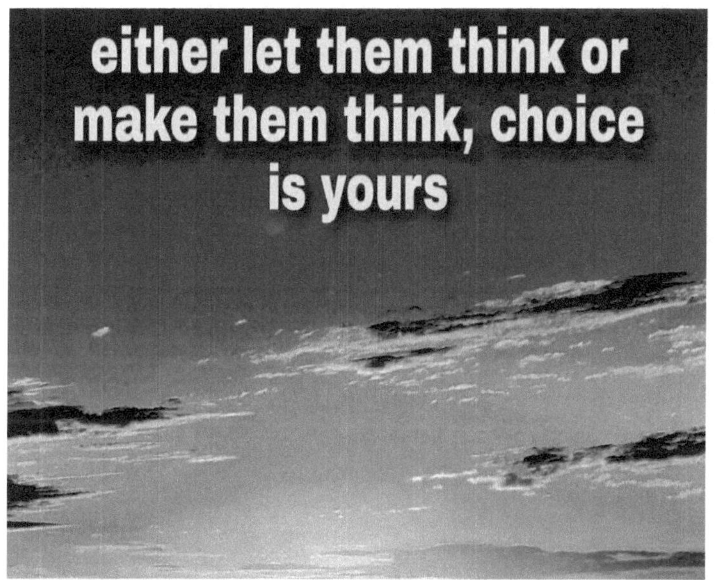
either let them think or
make them think, choice
is yours

either u get what
u expect or u get
what u accept

YOU CAN'T CREATE
REALITY,
YOU CAN ONLY
DISCOVER IT

EXPERIENCE
OUTPLAYS INTUITION

you will not be
remembered in terms
of who you are , you
will be remembered
by what you did.

you drag your past
and
your future drags you

fate knows no mercy
it only knows you

your expectations
reveal your character
much more than your
intentions.

truth and respect
hardly come
together.

Sometimes you have
to do it alone.
So that you learn
few more things

knowing your
mistake and
realising it are
two different
things.

Do the justice,
be in love rather than
asking for it.

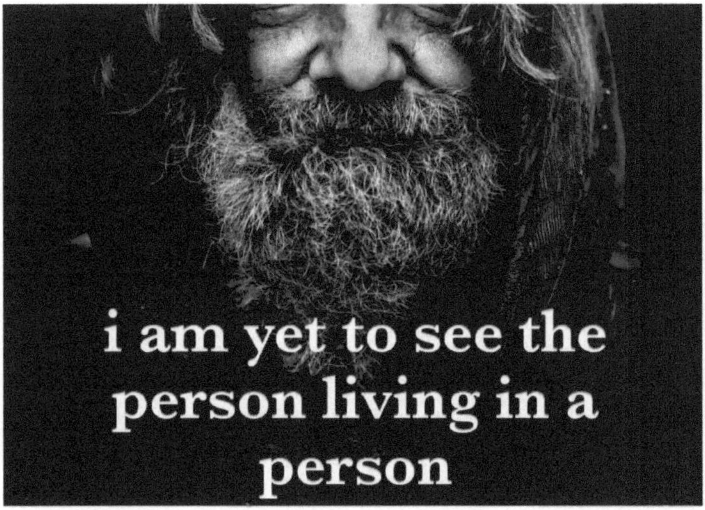

i am yet to see the
person living in a
person